DATE DUE		
JAN 14 2013		
		MAY 16 2013

The Urbana Free Library

To renew: call 217-367-4057
or go to "*urbanafreelibrary.org*"
and select "Renew/Request Items"

BOOKS IN THIS SERIES

Draw 50 Airplanes, Aircraft, and Spacecraft

Draw 50 Aliens, UFOs, Galaxy Ghouls, Milky Way Marauders, and Other
Extraterrestrial Creatures

Draw 50 Animal 'Toons

Draw 50 Animals

Draw 50 Athletes

Draw 50 Beasties and Yugglies and Turnover Uglies and Things That Go Bump
in the Night

Draw 50 Birds

Draw 50 Boats, Ships, Trucks, and Trains

Draw 50 Buildings and Other Structures

Draw 50 Cars, Trucks, and Motorcycles

Draw 50 Cats

Draw 50 Creepy Crawlies

Draw 50 Dinosaurs and Other Prehistoric Animals

Draw 50 Dogs

Draw 50 Endangered Animals

Draw 50 Famous Caricatures

Draw 50 Famous Cartoons

Draw 50 Famous Faces

Draw 50 Flowers, Trees, and Other Plants

Draw 50 Holiday Decorations

Draw 50 Horses

Draw 50 Monsters, Creeps, Superheroes, Demons, Dragons, Nerds, Dirts,
Ghouls, Giants, Vampires, Zombies, and Other Curiosa . . .

Draw 50 People

Draw 50 People of the Bible

Draw 50 Sharks, Whales, and Other Sea Creatures

Draw 50 Vehicles

DRAW 50 HOLIDAY DECORATIONS

DRAW 50 HOLIDAY DECORATIONS

LEE J. AMES
WITH RAY BURNS

BROADWAY BOOKS
New York

BROADWAY

Published by Broadway Books
a division of Random House, Inc.
1540 Broadway, New York, New York 10036

BROADWAY BOOKS and it's logo, a letter B bisected on the diagonal, are
trademarks of Broadway Books, a division of Random House, Inc.

Library of Congress Cataloging-in-Publication Data

Ames, Lee J.
    Draw 50 holiday decorations.

    Summary: Step-by-step instructions for drawing a
variety of holiday subjects such as Baby New Year, Cupid
and his arrow, July 4th rockets, turkey, pumpkin,
Easter basket, Santa Claus, and a menorah.
    1. Holiday decorations in art—Juvenile literature.
2. Drawing—Technique—Juvenile literature. [1. Drawing
—Technique. 2. Holidays in art]   I. Burns, Raymond,
1924–   II. Title. III. Title: Draw fifty holiday
decorations.
NC825.H65A44   1987   743′.87455941   87-15581
ISBN 0-385-19057-3
ISBN 0-385-19058-1 (lib.bdg.)
ISBN 0-385-26770-3 (pbk.)

19 18

To Ray Burns for a job well done

To the Reader

Holiday times are special times because they inspire us to be creative—to make things that will delight family and friends alike. Here is a book to help celebrate those special times. It will show you how to draw a variety of holiday subjects—a jack-o'-lantern for Halloween, a bunny for Easter, Santa Claus for Christmas, a menorah for Hanukkah, and much more. With these drawings, you can then decorate greeting cards, gift tags, place cards, party favors, and anything else you can think of. Or you may just want to draw the pictures for the fun of it.

At first glance, these drawings may appear difficult. But if you take your time and carefully follow the step-by-step instructions in each illustration, you will be able to produce a very satisfying finished drawing.

To begin, you will need only clean paper, a pencil with moderately soft lead (HB or No. 2), and a kneaded eraser (available at art supply stores). Select the illustration you want to draw, and then, *very lightly and carefully,* sketch out step number one. Then, also very *lightly and carefully,* add step number two to step number one. These steps, which may look the easiest, are the most important. A mistake here can ruin your entire drawing at the end. And remember to watch not only the lines themselves, but the *spaces between the lines* to make sure that they are the same as the drawing in the book. As you sketch out these first steps, it might be a good idea to hold your work up to a mirror. Sometimes the mirror shows that you've twisted the drawing off to one side without being aware of it.

In each drawing, the new step is shown darker than the previous one so that it can be clearly seen. But you should keep your own work very light. Here's where the kneaded eraser will come in handy; use it to lighten your work after each step.

When you have finished your picture, you may want to go over it with some India ink. Apply this with a fine brush or pen. When the ink has thoroughly dried, erase the entire drawing with the kneaded eraser. The erasing will not affect the India ink.

The most important thing to remember is that even if your first attempts are not as good as you would like them to be, you should not get discouraged. Like any other talent, whether it be performing gymnastic feats or playing the piano, drawing takes practice to do your best.

Though there are many ways to learn how to draw, the step-by-step method used in this book should start you off in the right direction.

LEE J. AMES

To the Parent or Teacher

"Leslie can draw a Halloween pumpkin better than anybody else!" Such peer acclaim and encouragement generate incentive. Contemporary methods of art instruction (freedom of expression, experimentation, self-evaluation of competence and growth) provide a vigorous, fresh-air approach for which we must all be grateful.

New ideas need not, however, totally exclude the old. One such is the "follow me, step-by-step" approach. In my young learning days this method was so common, and frequently so exclusive, that the student became nothing more than a pantographic extension of the teacher. In those days it was excessively overworked.

This does not mean that the young hand is never to be guided. Rather, specific guiding is fundamental. Step-by-step guiding that produces satisfactory results is valuable even when the means of accomplishment are not fully understood by the student.

The novice with a musical instrument is frequently taught to play simple melodies as quickly as possible, well before he learns the most elemental scratchings at the surface of music theory. The resultant self-satisfaction, pride in accomplishment, can be a significant means of providing motivation. And all from mimicking an instructor's "Do-as-I-do . . ."

Mimicry is prerequisite for developing creativity. We learn the use of our tools by mimicry. Then we can use those tools for creativity. To this end I would offer the budding artist the opportunity to memorize or mimic (rote-like, if you wish) the making of "pictures." "Pictures" he has been anxious to be able to draw.

The use of this book should be available to anyone who *wants* to try another way of flapping his wings. Perhaps he or she will then get off the ground when a friend says, "Leslie can draw a Halloween pumpkin better than anybody else!"

LEE J. AMES

DRAW
50
HOLIDAY
DECORATIONS

New Year's Day

New Year's Day

Martin Luther King, Jr.'s Birthday

Groundhog Day

Abraham Lincoln's Birthday

Abraham Lincoln's Birthday

Valentine's Day

Valentine's Day

Valentine's Day

George Washington's Birthday

George Washington's Birthday

St. Patrick's Day

St. Patrick's Day

Passover

Easter

Easter

Easter

Easter

Mother's Day

Flag Day

Independence Day

Independence Day

Independence Day

Independence Day

Labor Day

Yom Kippur/Rosh Hashanah

Columbus Day

Columbus Day

Halloween

Halloween

Halloween

Halloween

Halloween

Election Day

Veterans Day

Hanukkah

Christmas

Christmas

Christmas

Christmas

Christmas

Christmas

Christmas

Christmas

Christmas

Christmas

DRAW 50 FOR HOURS OF FUN!

Using Lee J. Ames's proven, step-by-step method of drawing instruction, you can easily learn to draw animals, monsters, airplanes, cars, sharks, buildings, dinosaurs, famous cartoons, and so much more! Millions of people have learned to draw by using the award-winning "Draw 50" technique. Now you can too!

COLLECT THE ENTIRE DRAW 50 SERIES!

The Draw 50 Series books are available from your local bookstore. You may also order direct (make a copy of this form to order). Titles are paperback, unless otherwise indicated.

ISBN	TITLE	PRICE	QTY	TOTAL
23629-8	Airplanes, Aircraft, and Spacecraft	$8.95/$13.95 Can	× _____ =	_____
49145-X	Aliens	$8.95/$13.95 Can	× _____ =	_____
19519-2	Animals	$8.95/$13.95 Can	× _____ =	_____
90544-X	Animal 'Toons	$8.95/$13.95 Can	× _____ =	_____
24638-2	Athletes	$8.95/$13.95 Can	× _____ =	_____
26767-3	Beasties and Yugglies and Turnover Uglies and Things That Go Bump in the Night	$8.95/$13.95 Can	× _____ =	_____
47163-7	Birds	$8.95/$13.95 Can	× _____ =	_____
47006-1	Birds (hardcover)	$13.95/$18.95 Can	× _____ =	_____
23630-1	Boats, Ships, Trucks, and Trains	$8.95/$13.95 Can	× _____ =	_____
41777-2	Buildings and Other Structures	$8.95/$13.95 Can	× _____ =	_____
24639-0	Cars, Trucks, and Motorcycles	$8.95/$13.95 Can	× _____ =	_____
24640-4	Cats	$8.95/$13.95 Can	× _____ =	_____
42449-3	Creepy Crawlies	$8.95/$13.95 Can	× _____ =	_____
19520-6	Dinosaurs and Other Prehistoric Animals	$8.95/$13.95 Can	× _____ =	_____
23431-7	Dogs	$8.95/$13.95 Can	× _____ =	_____
46985-3	Endangered Animals	$8.95/$13.95 Can	× _____ =	_____
19521-4	Famous Cartoons	$8.95/$13.95 Can	× _____ =	_____
23432-5	Famous Faces	$8.95/$13.95 Can	× _____ =	_____
47150-5	Flowers, Trees, and Other Plants	$8.95/$13.95 Can	× _____ =	_____
26770-3	Holiday Decorations	$8.95/$13.95 Can	× _____ =	_____
17642-2	Horses	$8.95/$13.95 Can	× _____ =	_____
17639-2	Monsters	$8.95/$13.95 Can	× _____ =	_____
41194-4	People	$8.95/$13.95 Can	× _____ =	_____
47162-9	People of the Bible	$8.95/$13.95 Can	× _____ =	_____
47005-3	People of the Bible (hardcover)	$13.95/$19.95 Can	× _____ =	_____
26768-1	Sharks, Whales, and Other Sea Creatures	$8.95/$13.95 Can	× _____ =	_____
14154-8	Vehicles	$8.95/$13.95 Can	× _____ =	_____
	Shipping and handling	**(add $2.50 per order)** ×	_____ =	_____
		TOTAL		_____

Please send me the title(s) I have indicated above. I am enclosing $_____.

Send check or money order in U.S. funds only (no C.O.D.s or cash, please). Make check payable to Random House, Inc. Allow 4–6 weeks for delivery. Prices and availability subject to change without notice.

Name: _____

Address: _____ Apt. #_____

City: _____ State: _____ Zip: _____

Send completed coupon and payment to:
Random House, Inc.
Customer Service
400 Hahn Rd.
Westminster, MD 21157

BROADWAY